S0-CIF-897

Table for Two

**an African folktale retold
by Pauline Cartwright
Illustrated by David Diaz**

CELEBRATION PRESS
Pearson Learning Group

Turtle was hot and tired and very hungry. He had walked long and far.

"I smell fish," he said. "I smell yams too." Turtle walked as fast as a turtle can to his friend Anansi's house.

Anansi heard Turtle's knock at the door. "Come in," said Anansi. "Come in and share my dinner."

Turtle smiled as he sat down at the table.

4

Now Anansi really didn't want to share his dinner with Turtle. He wanted the fish and yams all to himself, so he thought of an idea to trick Turtle.

Turtle was just about to reach for some food.

"Look at you," cried Anansi. "Your hands are dirty, Turtle! It's not polite to eat with dirty hands. Please go down to the river and wash up."

Turtle made his way down to the river at the bottom of the hill to wash up.

He washed carefully. "I've walked a long way today," he said to himself. "I'm very hungry."

Turtle walked as fast as a turtle can up the hill to Anansi's house.

When he reached the top, Turtle saw that Anansi had already eaten half of the meal. Turtle sat down to eat some fish and yams too.

"Turtle," cried Anansi, "your hands are still dirty! Please go back down to the river and wash up."

Turtle looked down at his hands. They were covered with dust from his walk up the hill.

Turtle went back down to the river to wash again. This time he was careful to crawl over the grass as he went up the hill.

When he got back to the table, Anansi was just finishing the last bite of food.

"I'm sorry," said Anansi. "I was so hungry. I just couldn't wait for you any longer."

Turtle sighed. He knew Anansi had tricked him. "Oh, well," said Turtle, "maybe you could have dinner with me tomorrow."

"That would be nice," said Anansi.

The next day, Anansi went to visit Turtle.

"Hello," said Turtle, popping out of the water.

"I've just put everything on the table. It's time for dinner. Come on down."

Then Turtle disappeared under the water.

Anansi jumped into the water, but he couldn't go under like Turtle. His legs were too thin and his body was too light. He floated on the top of the water.

Anansi said, "I need to make myself heavy."

Anansi quickly filled his jacket pockets with stones. Then down, down he went to the bottom of the pond.

What a meal Turtle had on his table!
"This looks great!" said Anansi, as he reached for some food.

"Not yet, Anansi," said Turtle. "It's not polite to eat with a jacket on. Please take it off."

Anansi slowly removed his jacket. As soon as he took the coat off, he floated back to the top of the water.

And Turtle sat at his table and ate the whole meal himself.